Creature of the Deep

By Jeri Cipriano

Scott Foresman
is an imprint of

Glenview, Illinois • Boston, Massachusetts • Chandler, Arizona • Upper Saddle River, New Jersey

Photographs

Every effort has been made to secure permission and provide appropriate credit for photographic material. The publisher deeply regrets any omission and pledges to correct errors called to its attention in subsequent editions.

Unless otherwise acknowledged, all photographs are the property of Pearson Education, Inc.

Photo locators denoted as follows: Top (T), Center (C), Bottom (B), Left (L), Right (R), Background (Bkgd)

Opener: (T) ©Christian Darkin/Photo Researchers, Inc.; **3** STF/AFP/Getty Images; **4** ©Jeffrey Rotman/Corbis; **5** (T) ©Christian Darkin/Photo Researchers, Inc.; **6** ©Tsunemi Kubodera of the National Science Museum of Japan, HO/©AP Photo; **7** (T) ©Clive Streeter/©DK Images; **8** ©Laurie O'Keefe/Photo Researchers, Inc.; **10** ©Richard Ellis/Photo Researchers, Inc.; **11** ©Christian Darkin/Alamy; **12** ©The Natural History Museum, London; **13** ©North Wind Picture Archives/Alamy Images; **14** AFP Photo/Tasmanian Museum and Art Gallery/Getty Images; **16** ©De Agostini Picture Library/Getty Images.

ISBN 13: 978-0-328-47290-1
ISBN 10:   0-328-47290-5

Copyright © by Pearson Education, Inc., or its affiliates. All rights reserved. Printed in the United States of America. This publication is protected by copyright, and permission should be obtained from the publisher prior to any prohibited reproduction, storage in a retrieval system, or transmission in any form or by any means, electronic, mechanical, photocopying, recording, or likewise. For information regarding permissions, write to Pearson Curriculum Rights & Permissions, One Lake Street, Upper Saddle River, New Jersey 07458.

Pearson® is a trademark, in the U.S. and/or in other countries, of Pearson plc or its affiliates.
Scott Foresman® is a trademark, in the U.S. and/or in other countries, of Pearson Education, Inc., or its affiliates.

3 4 5 6 7 8 9 10 V010 13 12 11 10

We all know there's no such thing as a sea monster, right? Still, a dangerous creature lives deep in the sea. It's the giant squid.

Scientists must dive in a submersible such as this one to study deep-sea creatures. Sometimes scientists take pictures by putting a camera on a heavy cable and lowering it to the ocean floor.

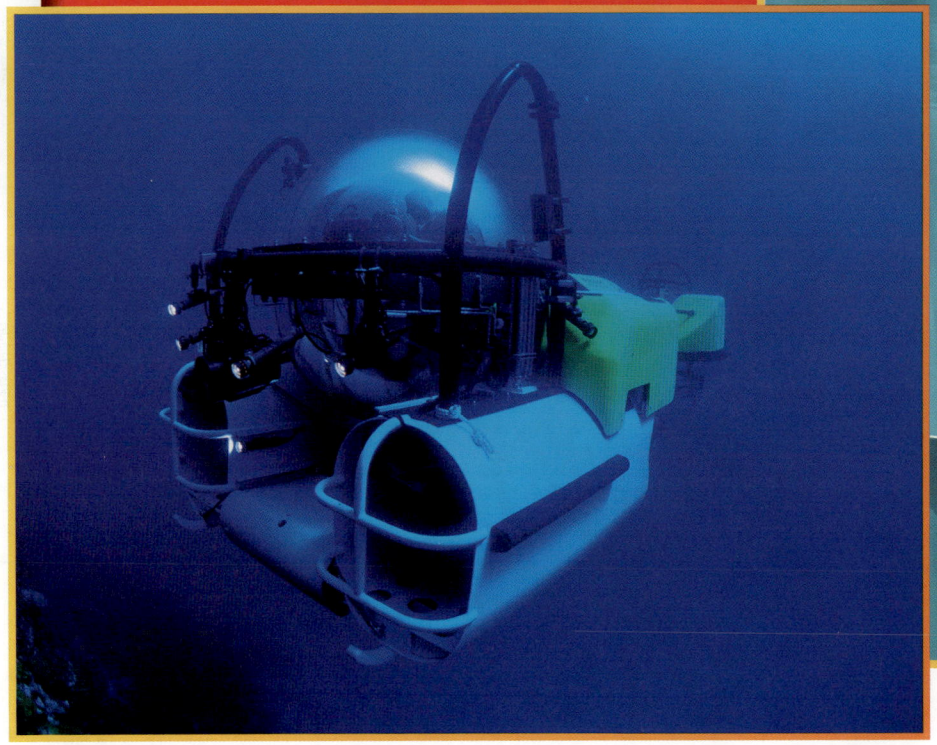

In 2004 the first live photographs of this predator were taken almost 3,000 feet beneath the sea. Giant squid live at a depth where no light can shine through—even during the day!

When a giant squid sees prey, it moves and strikes like a python. It uses its tentacles to grab the prey. Then it rolls it up in a ball before it tosses the prey into its beak-like mouth. Fish, shrimp, and other smaller squid go down in just a few gulps.

Giant squid can be between 25 and 40 feet long. That's longer than a school bus! They can weigh close to a ton. Their eyeballs are the largest in the animal kingdom. Each eye can be 18 inches across. That is larger than a basketball!

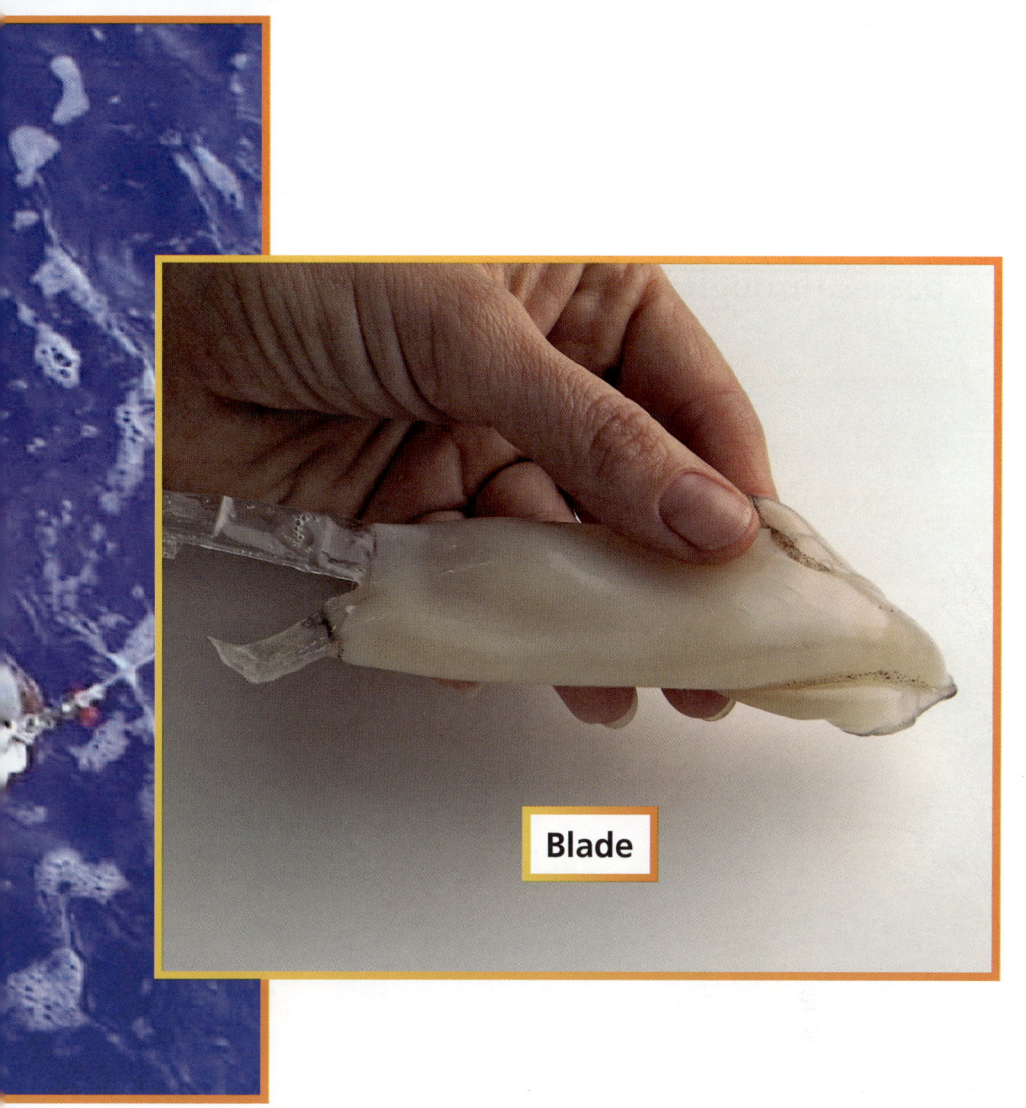

Blade

Squid are invertebrates. That means they have no bones. The giant squid is the largest invertebrate in the world. A feather-shaped blade supports the squid's body. The blade is made of a substance similar to your fingernail.

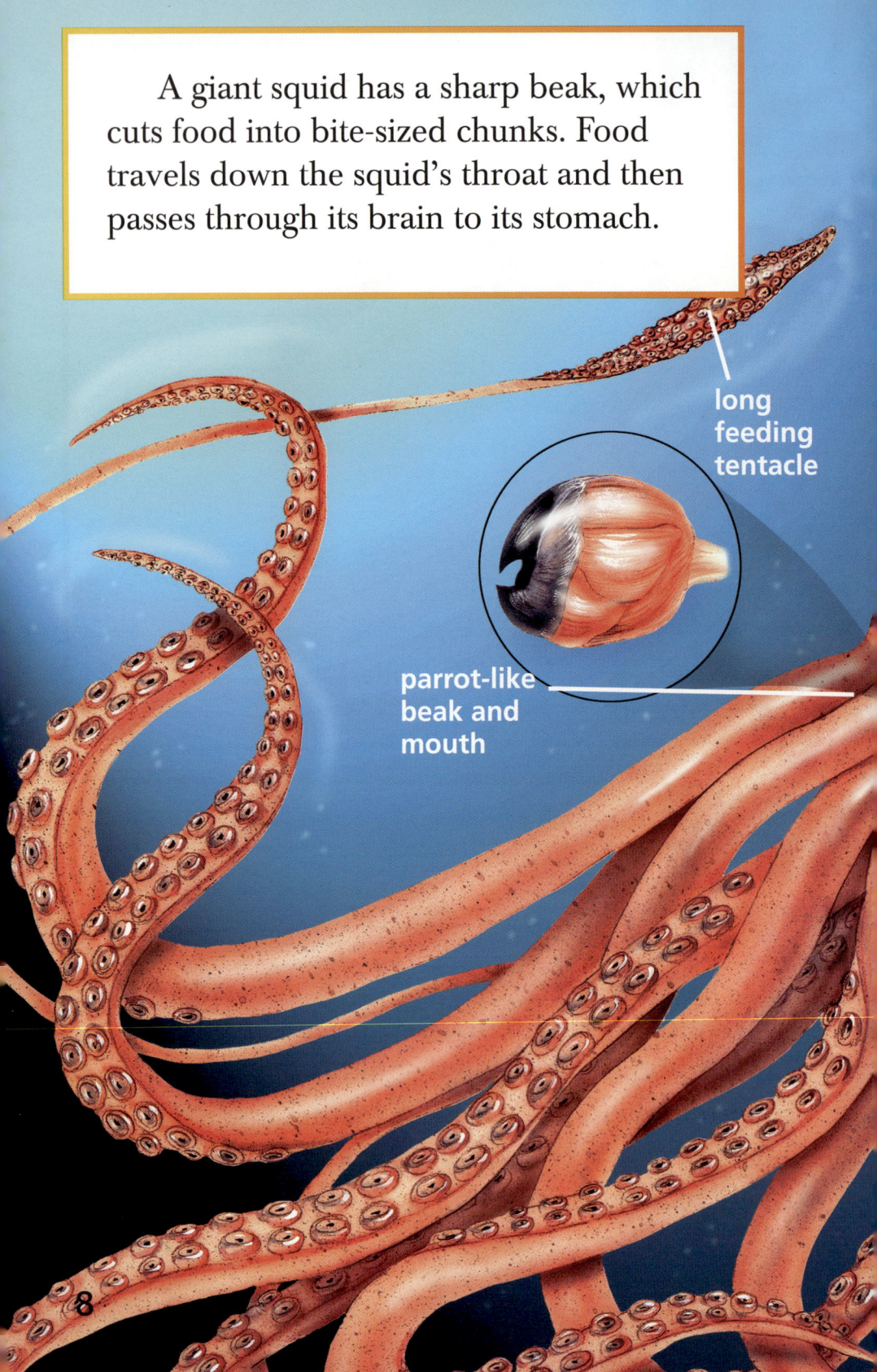

A giant squid has a sharp beak, which cuts food into bite-sized chunks. Food travels down the squid's throat and then passes through its brain to its stomach.

long feeding tentacle

parrot-like beak and mouth

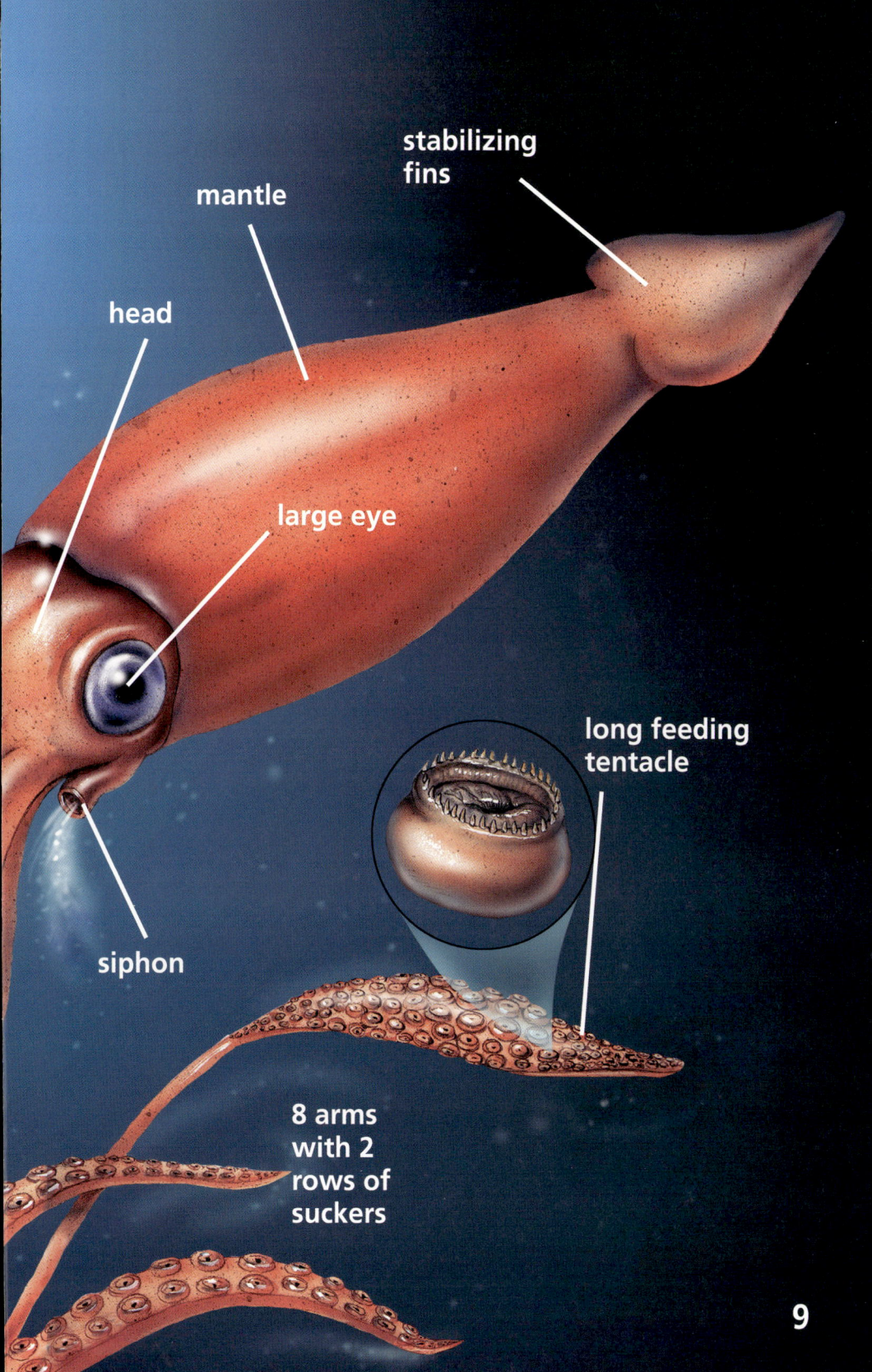

A squid's only enemy is the sperm whale. But the squid has a unique way of defending itself. It shoots out a big blob of black ink. Its enemy focuses on the ink blob. Meanwhile, the squid turns pale and swims away.

A giant squid and sperm whale in a fight to the death

Giant squid are built like torpedoes. They move through the water with a kind of jet propulsion.

The squid moves by squirting water from the *mantle* through the *siphon*.

The giant squid has eight long arms and two tentacles. The tentacles have hooks and suckers for latching onto prey. The squid's beak-like mouth is strong enough to cut through steel cable.

Detail of surface of tentacle

For years, stories were told about many-armed creatures that could pull whole ships down into the ocean. As far back as 1861, sailors tried to capture a real giant squid. It wasn't until recently that scientists were finally able to study and photograph the squid in its natural habitat.

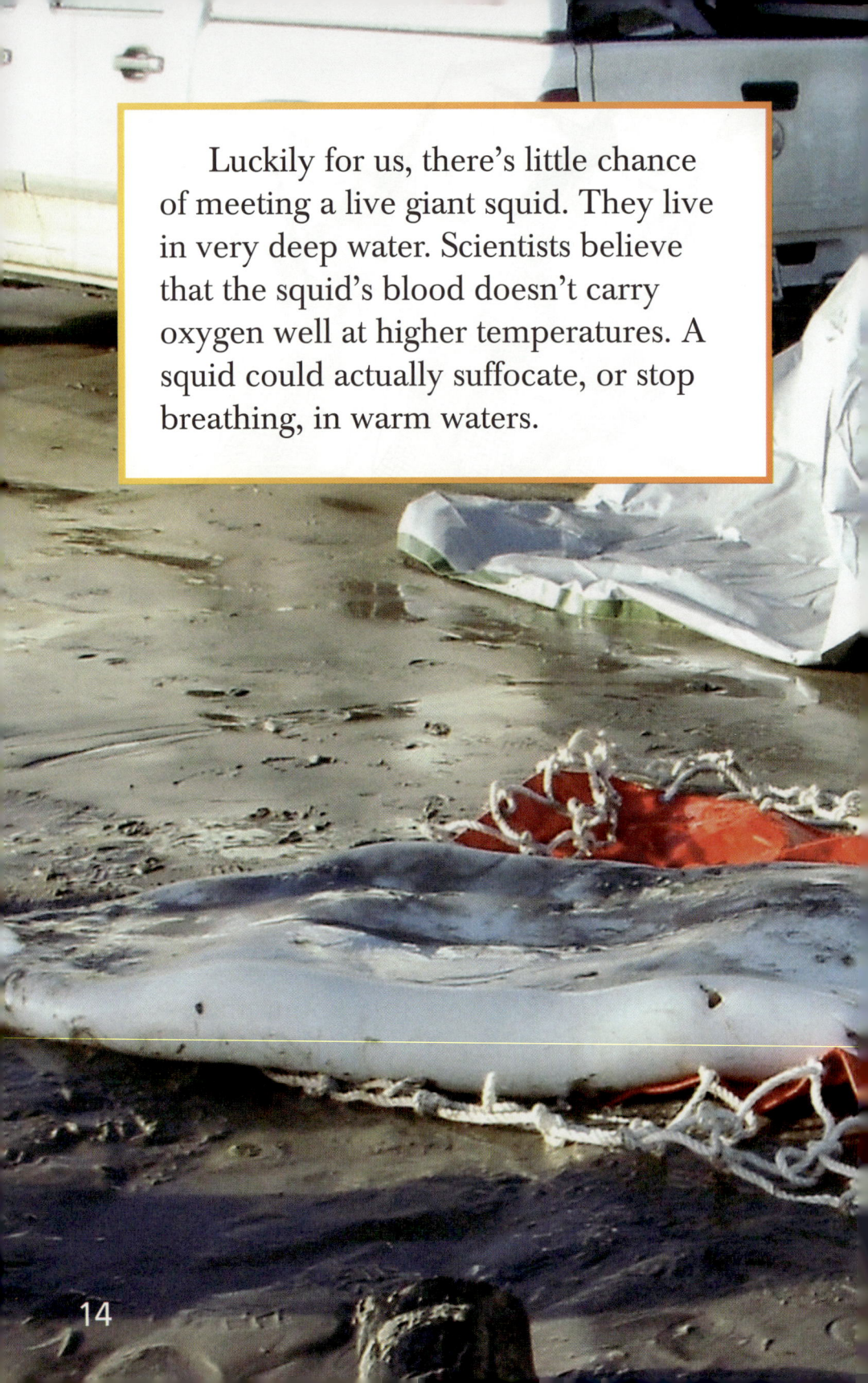

Luckily for us, there's little chance of meeting a live giant squid. They live in very deep water. Scientists believe that the squid's blood doesn't carry oxygen well at higher temperatures. A squid could actually suffocate, or stop breathing, in warm waters.

People sometimes find dead giant squids that have washed up on beaches.

There are about 500 kinds of squid, ranging from 1 inch to 60 feet long. Scientists still regard the giant squid as a great mystery of the deep because so few have ever been seen in their own habitat.

"Now that we know where to find them," one Japanese scientist said, "we think we can be more successful at studying them in the future."